REACH

for the

LIGHT

By
Ilana R. Lunn

ISBN: 978-0-9908615-3-9

Dedication
Greg Lunn
Beloved husband

Artist
W. James Blanford, Jr.

Special thanks
Cover design - Barr Batzer
Description - Marla Madden

TABLE OF CONTENTS

Empty Well 1

ACROSTICS

"Hosanna" 3

"Glory" 3

"Honor" 3

"Mighty" 4

"Mercy" 4

"Life" 4

"Power" 4

"Song" 5

"Glory" 5

"Play" 5

"Jesus" 5

"God" 5

"Worship-Praise" 6

"Forever" 6

"King" 6

"King" (2) 7

"Heaven" 7

"Pillow" 7

"Glass" 7

"David" 8

"Adam and Eve" 8

"Hope" 8

Hope 9

Journey 13

Are You There God? 19

Ungrateful Children 21

Rock of Salvation 23

One Creation 25

Life 27

Waiting 29

Quicksand 31

Bright Eyes 33

Only Time 35

Roots 37

Love So Simple 39

Listen Now 41

Peaceful Deception 43

Beyond Reason 45

Fork in the Path 47

Stop! 49

Wrong Help 51

I Need You 53

I Cannot Fathom 55

I Love Despite 57

Always Free 59

Just Look 61

Mindful Death 63

Chosen 65

The Vessel's Eyes 67

Scarlet 69

Heavenly Music 71

Shelter 73

Ladder of Hope 75

Seek Him 77

Divine Mercy 79

The Lost 81

Lost! 83

Pride 85

Sorrow to Grace 87

Opening My Eyes 89

The End 91

A Mothers Loss 93

The Pardon 95

The Deceiver 97

The Redeemer 99

Lost Child 101

Cry in Despair 103

New Day 105

Empty Well

I say the words
But my prayers are empty
I am but an empty bottle
Drained of its contents

Refill me Lord
You are my only source of nourishment

As a well runs dry
You are my fountain of life
Eternally flowing
Over the cliffs of my life

ACROSTICS

"Hosanna"

Holy art Thou
On the edge of clouds
Sailing through the stars
Atop the heavens
Never stopping
Nor ever far away
Always close to my heart

"Glory"

Glory be Your name
Lifting us up
Over the cares of this world
Reaching for heaven's glory
You embrace us

"Honor"

Holy be Your name
On the tips of our tongues
Never ceasing
On our lips eternal praise
Raising our eyes to heaven

"Mighty"

Mighty is our Lord
In His longsuffering love
Gliding through the heavens
High above the mountains
Telling us
Youth is eternal

"Mercy"

Maybe we are undeserving
Eternally damned
Reaching for worldly cares
Ceasing to live
Yet we are forgiven

"Life"

Living isn't worth much
In the day to day world
Flying on empty
Except for those who believe

"Power"

Pursuing a silver lining
On the clouds of our lives
Wondering where we are
Each of us will one day
Realize it's God

"Song"

Soft as a mother's whisper
Or loud as the morning rooster
Nothing shall ever stop us
God is our conductor

"Glory"

Glory be Your name
Lifting us up
Over the cares of this world
Reaching for heaven's glory
You embrace us

"Play"

Perfect is Your joy
Laughing all the time
Allowing us to sing
Your praises forever

"Jesus"

Just as a mother nurses her young
Empowering them with nourishment
So we too need our milk
Ever more so
Since we are helpless without it

"God"

Garbage and dung
Old sins and new
Destroyed by one mighty fist

"Worship-Praise"

Wrestling all our days
Overwrought with fear
Reeking of sin
Sinking to the black depths
Heads turn toward heaven
In voices they cry
Praises to the Mighty King

Praying for salvation
Realizing their wrongs
Addressing their only hope
In the Son of the Most Holy
Seeking His face
Eternal peace frees them at last

"Forever"

Fighting for our lives
Overcome with sorrow
Resigning in the last
Each of us finally turns
Verily I tell you
Each of you will turn
Residing in God's embrace

"King"

Kindhearted and fearsome
Insomuch as He loves us
Never to abandon His children
Guiding us to His throne

"King" (2)

Kindly and sweetly leading
Into His palace
New hopes arise
Guiding us ever closer to His light

"Heaven"

High above the mountaintops
Eternity
Awaits
Venting its light through the clouds
Each day
Nearer to our hearts

"Pillow"

Peaceful
Intoxicating
Loving
Life-giving
Omnipotent
Wrapped in His embrace

"Glass"

Gliding so delicately
Life finds a way
Always on the edge
Shattering the darkness
Setting us free

"David"

Devoted to God
Archaic in life
Victorious in battle
Immodest in character
Dedicated in faith

"Adam and Eve"

Amongst them all
Deemed special in His eyes
A being created in His image
Man came to life

Ashes fell upon his head
No longer was he close to His Creator
Directed out of His presence

Eternally separated
Vice died on the cross
Eternity washed away the ashes

"Hope"

Harrowing though it may be
Overtures of life
Press us on to live
Each day fervently praying

Hope

Grief, a void in my heart
Who can fill it?
Where is hope?
Am I alone
Or do others share?
I need you, Lord
Now more then ever
There is an emptiness
Within my soul
Only You can fill
Where did this hole come from?
I know all to well
Greif has bidden to my heart
Where are they, Lord?
Will I be with them again?
Are they with you?
Or in the miry depths?
Do those without faith
Have any hope?
Did she know you in the end?
I miss her terribly
My loving grandmother
Her love, her laughter
But she did not know you
She was so miserable, Lord
Unhappy with her life
But then joy came
That last week she was happy
Dying in peace
Did she come to know you
Or is she lost forever?
Is it to late to pray
All I can do is hope
And trust in Your love
What of animals?
Is Sammi happy now?
I like to believe
There is heaven for cats
It is comforting to think on

My pain grows deeper
Bonnie has gone before
These many years now
I remember the tears, the laughter
My twin, my best friend
She gave me confidence
When others criticized me
She suffered so much in this life
Yet she also found joy
Your Son was in her heart
Her hope was in Him
However she was blind
The full truth evaded her
Where is she, Lord?
Was her faith enough
Or did she go to the dark depth?
I am not sure, I lack confidence
Is she with you and my little ones?
All I can do is hope
I put my trust in You, O Lord
Now for my deepest grief, deepest pain
My innocent ones – Tina and Benjamin
How I miss them Lord
I wish I could have held them in my arms
As I do in my heart, in my soul
So painful to think about
Are there sufficient or adequate words
To express my grief, my loss?
I am totally alone, empty
A broken vessel
The pain is too much to bear
Yet the tears won't come
I want to cry, scream
But I cannot
They're buried deep within my soul
Where they will always be
Is my grief for them equal?
I feel grief for one
The other is numb, peaceful
I never grieved for Benjamin
The one You named for me
You brought peace to my soul

Saying, he is the son of Your right hand
I took comfort, peace of mind
Knowing he is safe with Jesus
However I never grieved for him
At least not that I'm aware of
I need closure, Lord
Do I have to wait till I die?
Hope comforts me
One day he will be in my arms
In the meantime I live day to day
Knowing they are both with you
My little Tina with Benjamin
I have grieved her loss so much, Lord
Only You know, only You can share
How deep my grief goes
Do I have any tears left?
I want to hold her in my arms
But she was not meant to be
You took her away, Lord
My pride and joy, my hope in life
Years have come and gone
My pain has lightened slowly
I know she is with Jesus
He watches over my babies
Until the day I die
Till I am with them myself
Why did Bonnie get to die before me?
I want to die, Lord
The pain is too much
It hurts me physically
I want my babies back
Please, Lord, give me hope
Show me I'll never be alone
They are always with me
I can't stand it any longer
I remember the peace when Jeanie died
She lay there, looking so small and frail
Yet I felt such overwhelming, perfect peace
I want the peace, Lord
Jeanie is watching over my babes
This I know to be true
Her suffering ended, she went to be with you

I want to be with you, Lord
I'm tired of life on Earth
The pain is overbearing
Send me hope, joy in this life, Lord
Don't let me be alone
Bless my womb, please
No more pain, no more sorrow
I want to laugh and cry again
I want to feel life, be life
Closing my eyes I try to be still
You are my hope, my refuge
My only hope, Savior
Bless me, Lord
Keep me as a babe in Your arms
I will always look to You for hope

Journey

Anger
Beset by grief
Spirals downward
Into darkness' void
Blinding truth
A path to peace
Hung all about
Groping for a hold
Bu nevertheless failing
Grasping threads
Torn by thorns
Killing the roses
Red, white, black
All occasions
Sickly faces
Confined by fear
Covering eyes
Do not look
Upon death's face
You are alone
You are nothing
"Come with us"
They beckon
Hide in there
No one will find you
Ever again
Hide from the great eye
He will not find you
Amongst the rubble
Your soul has sunk
Into quagmires too deep
For escape
"Take our hand"
They cry out
Cover your ears
You don't need them
All are against you
Steel clings on steel
Ringing, clamoring

All is alive
All is dead
Hither yourself
Unto death
She's calling to you
Resistance breaking
Fall into her embrace
Yes that's it
Don't let go
Deeper, deeper
Into despair's pit
Resting in quicksand
Mud coats you
Feet to neck
Choking, illuminating
You do not belong here
But it is too late
She's caught you
Escape impossible
Soul quenched
Fire burns your face
Your very soul
He'll never find you here
Voices cry out
"We belong together"
Screaming tortures
Never ending pain
Just sink deeper, deeper
This is grief
Out of control
Nevertheless you try
Gazing upward
Taking a chance
Is that a light
A pin in the sky?
Keep looking
It becomes blinding
Painful tears
Pouring uncontrollably
The grief is too much
Your strength is gone
Hope is lost

There never was hope
Misery is your life
Your name
"Come take my hand"
A voice says in the void
You have no choice
She grasps you
Not letting go
Laughter sounds
Wicked and senile
Try to shake loose
Her hold is tight
Melodious singing
Birds above
Is that hope
Ringing above your head?
Soaring closer, closer
Black shapes
Winging down
Vultures come for your soul
All is lost
Come now
You set the trap
Never letting go
Allowance has cost you
Eternity in heaven
Darkness spills
Flooding your feet
Your very soul
There's the pin of light again
Reach for it
Just one more time
Grasping, it pokes
Excruciating pain

Overwhelming
Is that blood?
It hurts so much
The pin is too painful
Reaching deep down
Piercing your soul
Offering hope, forgiveness

But you cannot bear it
Thorns sprout
Upon the pin
Clouding the light
Fear within cries out
Let it go
Release the pin
The light closes in
Blood pours down
Drenching you
All is red, white
Darkness is fading
Kneeling in a quagmire
You cry out
The pain is too much
Alone and desolate
You cry in the darkness
Murky with blood
A hand reaches down
Grasping you
But she still holds you
A tug of war begins
Which way should you go
Where is the hope, the truth?
On your knees
Praying for release
Grips tighten
Black, white
Fighting over your very soul
Blinded by a red haze
Your head swims
Giving up
The rag doll falls
Held up by mere threads
Black, white, red
Whimpering, whispering
"Someone help me"
The light strengthens
Begins pulling up
Darkness cries out
"No, she's mine!"
Red rain pours

Delicate hands
Upon your face
Daring to look up
You gaze upon a white rose
Sitting atop the pin
You reach for it
Grasping a thorn
It is painful
A voice encourages you
Pushing on, strengthened
Climbing the pin
Light shining above
Thorn by thorn you climb
Unbelievable pain
Sight a red haze
Darkness tightens its grip
A hand slips
Hanging by a thread
The light beckons
Hope strengthens you
Fighting darkness
You clasp the thorns
Once more
Screeching in pain
Hand over hand
Light increases
Black loses its grip
Crying out angrily
Other pins, other roses appear
They are all around
You're not alone
More like you
Climbing thorns
Seeing each other
Through the red haze
Words echo all around
"You can do it"
Your resolves strengthens
Up and up, higher and higher
Until suddenly
The thorns are gone
Your sight clears

The white rose envelopes you
Darkness is out of sight
Relief, glowing relief
Healing grief, pain
Lighter and lighter
Your burden dissipates
Laughter rings out
Surprised, you realize
It was you
Hands reaching out
Touching others
Arriving from the same journey
Eternity is light
Darkness lost
It screams in anger
But you no longer hear it
Musical voices
Wings of light
Forever free
Encompassing peace
Breaks all dark threads left
You are no longer alone
You never were

Are You There God?

So far away
Yet within my reach
Why can't I touch you?
Are you there God?
Please guide me
Touch my soul
And lift me up
Beyond my imaginings
Limited to my morality
That you've blessed me with
In this harsh and dark world

Are you there God?
Touch me
And lift my soul
Out of this rotting decaying body
I need you Lord so much
To reach out and
Grab me

Pluck me out of this jungle
Called mankind
Fill me up with laughter
No more joy is in my heart

Oh Lord I beseech you!
Grasp my soul
With your mighty hands
And release me into paradise

Ungrateful Children

My lovely children
How I love you so

Why do you rebel?
Why do you turn your backs?

It breaks My heart so
To see My gifts tossed away

You laugh at My word
Mocking your creation

I sacrificed My Son for you
What else could you desire?

My heart aches from your wicked ways
Oh why won't you come home?

Rock of Salvation

Empty and alone
I stood
In a deep pit
Slipping deeper
And deeper
Every day

Until I looked up
Slowly raising my arm
My hand touched the air
Reaching for the clouds

A great hand grasped mine
Pulled me out of my pit
And set me on a firm rock
That has never faltered
Beneath my feet

One Creation

Girls and boys
Young and old
Black and white
Short and tall
Thin and plump
Rich and poor

No matter who you are
Or what you are

No matter where've you been
Or where you are now

No matter how compassionate
Or how heartless you are

No matter if you're wise or foolish
Or if you're simply ignorant

No matter how much you've sinned

I love you all

Life

Choices
We all make them
Every day
So many choices
In everything we do

We all have different choices to make
But there is one we all must make
At the beginning and at the end
In the midst of all the choices we make
Only one truly matters
A choice we all must face

Before Judgment Day

Waiting

How long My child?
I greet you every morning
With the rising sun
I watch you all day
Walking in the darkness
Listening for the words
I long to hear
Another day draws to its end
Your eyes never even glanced
I tuck you in
Under the night sky
Hoping
Maybe tomorrow
You will look towards me

Quicksand

Worries and woes
Darkness
Sins of our hearts
Drowning
Choking
Yet we continue to sin
Spiraling down
Deeper and deeper
Into darkness we fall

We must grasp for the light
Before it is too late

Bright Eyes

Child of the dark
You need only to open your eyes
To see the light

There is nothing to fear
Love like you've never known before
Shall embrace you

Peak through your tears
Let His love comfort you
And brighten the rest of your days

Come, open your eyes
Never be alone again
Join the children of the light

Only Time

Pain
Excruciating
Digging at my heart
Clutching at my soul
In its deepest depth

Will it ever be gone?
Will time be there for me?

Only You oh Lord
Can stop the pain
Only You can break the sword
Constantly stabbing me

How long must I wait?
Only time with You
Can heal my deepest wounds
I fall to my knees
Crying out in pain
To my Comforter

Roots

The time will come
When we will all be one
Our roots will become so entwined
Creating one root
That is the tree of life

Love So Simple

Why is it so difficult?
Is your heart that hard,
Your mind so blind,
Your spirit so dead?
Why so bitter to the
Utter depths of your soul?
You will never understand
Unless you open up
And learn to love
Is that so difficult?
Take my hand
I will show you
But your eyes must be open
Else I cannot help you
You must step forward
Be willing to share
Or your death will become
Permanent

Listen Now

Are you so stubborn?
Do you not yet hear -
Or are you refusing to listen?
Turn your ears to his voice
He is speaking to you
Every day
Every hour
Every minute
Yet you still do not hear
Your pride blinds you
Sinking into depths so deep
You cannot fathom your end
Eternally apart from His voice
And His presence.

Peaceful Deception

Strung up
All in a line
Blowing in the wind
Beautiful scenery
Fragrant nature
Sky so blue, grass so green
Life is perfect
But over the horizon
Dark clouds approach
A storm is brewing
Threatening the peace of
Your little world.
It will overtake you
Drench you in its stinging rain
No more beauty
No more fragrance -
Except that of burning flesh.
Put the armor on now, or
Suffer for all eternity

Beyond Reason

Confusion sets in
Where am I going?
Imaginations overwhelm me
I am bombarded with lies
From all directions
My mind is warped beyond comprehension
Who can take it away,
Who can still my soul?
I know where to go
But my heart, my mind are
Distracted beyond reason
There is no clarity of thought
Just a jumble of fantasies
Keeping me from peace, from God
I do not like this in myself
Make it go away
Help me, I need you
Heal my mind, my heart,
My imaginations

Fork in the Path

Delusions, delusions
Choices to make
Roads to follow
Paths to tread
Forks in the highway
Which way is right?
To this, or to that?
Narrow or high?
Wide or low?
Take the safer route,
If you know which it is
Trust in the Spirit
To guide you
Even when you don't want to
Finding yourself going
In the wrong direction
You - I - cry in earnest
Protect me!
Keep me from wrongdoing
Lead me to Your path of
Righteousness
Narrow and high, but
Safe.

Stop!

Don't do it
It won't solve anything
Turn away
You know it's wrong
Others can - will - help you
God will help you
Just ask
Stay away from the prince
His ways are evil
Selfish, pure deceit
Turn away now
Before regret overwhelms you
In the end
You must make a choice
Obey the King, or
Worship the prince
There is no between
It is one or the other
Listen to reason,
The Holy Spirit
Turn away
Before its too late

Wrong Help

It won't do any good
Only bring more harm
You belong to the Lord
Your body belongs to Him
Do not desecrate His temple
He'll see you through
All your fears and worries
Lay them at His feet
He can relieve your load
Lessen your pain
The prince will not help
But further destroy
Your true Prince will hold you
All you need to do is
Pray, trust - have faith
So don't do it
Instead, turn to the One
Who can - and will - help you
Cry your heart out
If that's what it takes
Bring it to the Lord
Before you regret any action

I Need You

How can I?
I am only human
I am nothing
Without you,
What am I?
I'm lost
I am blind
Where am I, O Lord
I need Your guidance
Your voice inspires me
In you I am content
You enable me to live
On earth and beyond
How can I?
Through Your love and mercy

I Cannot Fathom

I don't understand
How can this be?
You died for us -
You died for me
Love so powerful
Beyond human comprehension
I cannot fathom
The mercy and grace
You poured forth
Through Your sacrifice
I do not try to understand
I simply accept it
In all humility
And believe

I Love Despite

I love You O Lord
From deep in my heart
You penetrate me
Nothing is hidden from Your eyes
You know me
And yet You love me
Through all my weaknesses
And despite my sinful nature
You love me O Lord
You spread Your arms wide
"I love you, my child
Be at peace"

Always Free

Spare me your ridicule
Your lies, your deceit
I am no fool
And will not be fooled
I am His child
And He is my Father
Bombard me with all your darts
For you shall not defeat me
My Savior protects me
In the end you will be gone
And I will go home to Him.
So spout off all you want
Though your torture me day and night
Deep down I know the truth
And the truth shall free me from your chains
Imprison me in a cell, and
I will still be free
My spirit belongs to my Father
Not you, my tormentor
Be gone I say and leave me be.

Just Look

He is not here,
He is not there,
He is not anywhere
But He is everywhere
Just look around
You cannot miss Him
Wouldn't it be great to
Have Him within You?
You know it's possible
A choice must be made
Prince of this world, or
God within
He will protect you, sustain you
Through all the princely trials
Thrown at you
Trust, have faith
That still, small voice in there
Not here,
Not there,
But everywhere within

Mindful Death

Anger, secrets
Can I hold them in forever?
Torturous thoughts
Attacking me from all sides
Where do I turn?
Where can I hide?
There is no escape
Except through death
Going home at last
Where my mind will be
Safe for eternity
Yes, that is what I want
To go home,
To be with my Savior,
My God
Through Him I can overcome
This thought life of mine and
Be at peace in His loving arms

Chosen

Who can see, who can hear
Who will dare speak of it?
None but the chosen
Silver and gold they are
All to dear to let go
Where are they going,
When will they arrive?
Tomorrow approaches
The day is dying
Yesterday is in tatters
Listen up quick
Jump for joy all who sing
All who are lost
For you will be found
When you can see,
When you can hear
When you dare speak of it
From your heart
Deep within your soul
Lifting you out of the pit
Into eternal arms
Become the chosen
Of the Lord

The Vessel's Eyes

Gorgeous
Yes you are
Don't argue with me
Perfection escapes you
As it escapes all of us
But you are a beautiful being
A diamond in God's eye
Sparkling gems at his feet
Rubies we are at the cross
We were dirt and mud
He refined us - refined you
To Him, you are wondrous
Do you dare argue with Him?
We have no place in
Judging ourselves through
Our own eyes
So do not be blind
But look above and within
God says you are very good
As you are

Scarlet

Scarlet bulrushes
Dotting the horizon
Violet trees
Shading the perimeter
The universe is ours
All in all
Basket in basket
So run free
No one can hold you back
Scarlet lavender
Violet heather
So fragrant, so sweet
Imagine heaven
A paradise, an Eden
Just hold onto the scarlet rose
It is the key to eternity

Heavenly Music

Harmony's bounty
Soft notes gliding
Gentle, caressing
Music in the breeze
Come high, come low
Always a song
In my heart of hearts
A tune plays
Soothing my spirit
Bringing me to God
God's lyrics carry me
Through the roller coaster
Heaven is just after
That next hill

Shelter

Run along little doggy
There's no food here
No sustenance abounds
The clouds are rolling in
Dark and ominous
So run, run fast
Before the shards fall
Seek shelter quickly
But do not tremor
It's on a hill
Secure from the world
The windows are locked
Do not knock
But simply enter
The door will shut
After you're safe
In His arms

Ladder of Hope

Stand by me and see
There is no other path
The pits go deep, deeper
Darker and darker they grow
Light emanates waywardly
Follow the path
You will be blind

There is a ladder of hope
Standing straight in the jungle
Through the lofty clouds above
Reach up, reach high
Climb until you tire
Falling now

A great hand grabs your wrist
Pulling you up
Grab onto the ladder now
He won't let you fall again

Seek Him

Mercy
Everlasting…ever loving
A splendid heart
None can conceive
Pure and perfect
A snow dove
Born in the wastelands
Pining away
Cherishing
Every bit of life
Strangling….holding on
To all that is dear
Is there hope
For the lost…For lorn?
Always!
Seek Him first…now
And forevermore
The uppermost reaches
Are not high enough
For His dwelling
Seek Him
Young lovers…
Lovers of the soul…
Lovers of life
Forever and evermore
Grace abounds
In each of us
Pure and perfect
Love binds us
Two swans a-swimming
Circling miracles
Reflected in glass
Broken…but not
Beyond repair
"Come to me," He beckons
Perfect peace

A rainbow of doves
Taking flight
Everlasting arms
Await you
In the recesses
Of life

Divine Mercy

Load your burdens
Upon my feet
Drench my fingers
With your tears
For one at a time
You will be healed
Driving the wolves away
Into the forest
Deep in the fiery pit
Gaze at the rainbows
Let the waters
Glide down your body
See how refreshing
Reflected love is
Within the heart
Aching and alone
No more
The abuse stops here…
Now
At my feet
Wallow in your fears
No more
Safety is key
And I am
Perfect safety
I will not harm
As others have
Let My arms
Embrace you
Drench you
In living waters
On this side
Of Heaven
Where morals abound
And sin is no more
So let go

There is hope…
Freedom even
Just come to me
I'll keep the wolves away
Keep you tucked
In My wings
Forever

The Lost

Strangers amidst strangers
Blind among the deaf
The unyielding bellow
Their cries....
Outrage!
But for some…
The very few –
All is not well
Upon this earth
Hypocrisies…idiocies
Cry…demand!
Unabashed
All for naught
For where will they go
When all is said
And done?
Nowhere.
Deep darkness
Deeper than the imagination
Oh wayward souls,
Fools!
Will you never learn?
Set your sights above
Not the blind below
Open your ears
Before it's too late
"Come, all ye faithful"
Sing for the dammed
Let them hear
Angelic voices
Soothe them
With words of love
And grace and mercy
Offer forgiveness
To those without heart
For all their outcries

Words are empty
Futile
Come, flavor them
With true life
True love
True eternity

Lost!

Woe is me!
All is forgotten
Lost
Who am I
What am I
Past…present…
Future
I say it again:
Woe is me!
Such power was mine
I controlled so much….
So many!
Could have
Owned them all
But no
One mistake
One slip of the foot
I soaked in
The salt of the world
Now I lay
Drenched in drudge
Alone- a fool!
Too much…too many
Too quickly lost
A wrenched pity
No, do not
Look upon me
Hives and boils
Corrode my body
Cancer eats
At my brain…my heart
My very soul
Nothing is left
I am nothing
But a slug
Curses rain upon me

I had an empire!
All in ruins now
All have turned their backs
What is left for me?
Is there no hope?...Wait!
-What is that
Still small voice
I hear?

Pride

Line them up
All nice and neat
Prim and proper
Aren't we cozy?
Savor the relish
Sprinkle the herbs
Dance with joy
But oh don't you
Get on your knees –
You'll mess up
Your clothes
Clean and ironed
Just for this day
Have to look just right
The prince is coming!
Didn't you hear?
You must be perfect
Check your appearance…
Your attitude
Put the right face on
Remember –
Remember your good deeds
Point them out
Ever so clearly
A little sin here…
A little sin there…
Dust under the rug
Surely He won't look there!
He is ecstatic
To behold us!
How could He not –
Why, look at us!
Perfect – just like Him!
Remove the lint
From your clothes –
There you go

What? What plank?
There is no plank
In my eye!
Why is it so dark…
So hot…so empty…
So alone…?

Sorrow to Grace

Rain
It pours fire
Upon my soul
Burning sulfur
Suffocating embers
Embrace me
Enfolding its arms
Dragging me down
Forever down…
Is there no end
To this torment?
Lightning flashes
Crush my heart
Thunder pounds
In my head
Tragedy, I beseech you!
Take me…
A lowly being
A nothing
Cursed be my name
Blessing be my curse
Aghast
I stand still
On cliffs
Rimming the pit
Rocks inviting
My blood…
My very being
What point is there?
Death is death
Extreme to extreme
Sobbing…sobbing
I fall to my knees
Crying…wailing
When? Why?
Please…now!

Is that a soft breeze
Brushing my cheek
Ever so gently
Lifting me away?
Is it possible?
Is it true?
I'm safe
At last!

Opening My Eyes

Alas, my child
Come hither
Away from that manger
All stench and dirt
Nothing will come
Of that babe
Don't dirty yourself
Mud will cling
Weighing you down
Unpresentable you'll be
Worry not about
The babes mother
She is young and strong
Pay them no heed
The temple awaits
Sacrifices to be made
They are peasants
Come along!
Why do you stay
My child?
Nothing special here
Must I take you
By the hand?
Off your knees!
Your hands too?
What has gotten
Into you
You little fool?
I am not a fool!
All I see are
Poor peasants
And stinky animals.
Now come, before
The star in the sky
Completely blinds me!
Fine, I shall kneel

With you and
Gaze upon the babe
What is this?
A stirring in my soul
Blessed life
Before my eyes
Forgive me!

The End

Dear one
Fly away home
Higher and higher
Away from flames
The world burns
Smelling
Sulfur and ash
Inhaling the lost
And bereft
They think they can
Take the heat
But they know
Nothing
Cold wintery frost
Resides on the earth
So cold and
Refreshing…until
The heat wave
Eternal fury
No more control
No more laughter
No more choices
The end is come
Doves are gone
Lilies and swans
Eagles soar above
Heading for new land
It's not too late
If you take off now
Follow the
Rainbow promise
To the ultimate
Garden of milk and honey
No more fire, no burning
Ever blue above
Ever green

Where we walk
Go to Him
Little one
He has already
Made a place for you
Within His heart.
Hurry, now.

A Mothers Loss

Suffering long
Through the night
I cry out
In agony
Blind stabbing pain
Jarring my nerves
Barely moving
Lifting my eyes
Wailing
"Why, God? Why?"
Oh, how I loved him
Adored him
My arms ache
In loving
For just a moment
To hold him
Close to my heart
In this so-called
Physical material world
He was real
Oh so real
Deep swelling pain
Overwhelms me
My senses alive…
Yet dead
I ask "why" again…
Again and again
But no answer comes
In grief
I collapse
Hopeless…helpless
A fool
Lost…he's lost
Is this the end?
Nothing more?
But no…

A glimmer has appeared
Before my eyes
A voice so tender
Gentle and inviting
"You will hold him
In eternity
As a mother should"

The Pardon

Spritzes of flame
Shoot up
Burning all in sight
And within
It reaches
Into every soul
Living or dead
Crushing hopes…dreams
Eternity
Spilling into the night
Lava covers the land
Through the dark mists
And under the sun
Endless nightmare
Screams of anguish
Burnt but whole
Eaten yet starving
Is there any end
To this torment?
Take this cup
Far away
I will not drink
Its poison
Toxicity is my blood
Death to all
Who come near
And touch me
Rattling the cell bars
Of my self-appointed
Dungeon
I wait in agony
Screaming for help…
For a savior
Will no one aid me?
Is there one?
Who is that?

What is that light?
A key!
He is setting me
Free
I fall to my knees
Grateful beyond words
For my cry was heard
And answered

The Deceiver

Superimposed will
He will not relent
Never letting down
His guard
Seeking innocence
To kill
In one fell swoop
Easy prey
The little ones
New ones
Just born
A little deception here
Twisting truth there
It's all attitude now
Despondency…regret
Doubt
Edging abuse
Tickling mortality
Shredding modesty
Instigating
Absolving the guilty
Trampling pure souls
He whispers to those
Who will listen
"Self…self…self"
Oh run from him
While you still can
Cling to the savior
Ignore the lies
Embrace love…
Love of others
Savior's love
Unconditional…selfless
Black…gray…white
There is no grey
He is darkness

Always setting traps
True light –
Exposes them
Carrying you
Safely to His arms
Out of the enemy's
Reach.

The Redeemer

Alone, so alone
Darkness overwhelms
Silence reigns supreme
Clouds blaspheme
The sky above
Traps, pits
Falling, falling
All around
Slipping into nothingness
Fire consumes
My soul
Retching, burning
Walking coals
Rolling about
Path so straight
Yet crooked
Mortified
My soul burns
Envious for peace
Alluring
Out of reach
Yet in sight
Teasing, tempting
Light withdraws
Not deserved
Punishment reigns
Supreme
He laughs
A raucous sound
Haunting
Darkest of souls
No hope
No glory
No relief
Light beckons
Arms outstretched

A hand
I see a hand
Reaching down
Lighting the clouds
Climbing the ladder
I am grabbed
Pulled to safety
Forever, evermore

Lost Child

Despondent
I cry
Through the night
No moon
No stars
Just darkness
Black depths
Within my soul
Yearning
Yearning for peace
Dying, dying
My heart retches
Spoils of fun, joy
No laughter
Nevermore
Empty arms
All I see
Music fades
In the distance
Why, oh why
I cry out
Why me?
Why my child?
She is gone
Never to be seen
Never held
Will hope deign me
Hopeless, helpless?
Facing heaven
Facing God
I scream
Overwhelming
Pain, anger
Where is my child,
Your blessing?
Am I cursed,

Alone forever
Eyes dim
Tears brimming
I fall
To my knees
O help me, Jesus!
Help me!

Cry in Despair

Help me, Jesus
Guide me
My soul aches
With longing
Bless me,
Bless me already?
Forever empty
Hope dismissed
Help me now
I cry out
Disdaining you
Deceived
Forgotten
Forsaken
Colors so dark
No yellow, no white
No light shines
Gray, no black
Clouds arise
Dimming my life
Why?
I want to know
I deserve
To know
You turned your back
On me
Letting go
Falling, falling
Into despair
Never-ending pit
Empty arms
Cry out, scream
"Bless me!"
Will you not
Hold me?
Beckon your angels

Hold me up
I need you
Like never before
Crashing face down
Covered
In ashes
O won't you bless me
Blessed One?

New Day

Today is the day
A day of new dawning
No more sorrow
No more tears

Will you join me?
Never again will you be alone
My brothers and sisters

See how He comforts us
In all our days of labor
Come, lift your chin up high
A new day has dawned